POEMS FOR CHILDREN BY

Jane Yolen

Water Music

PHOTOGRAPHS BY

Jason Stemple

Wordsong / Boyds Mills Press

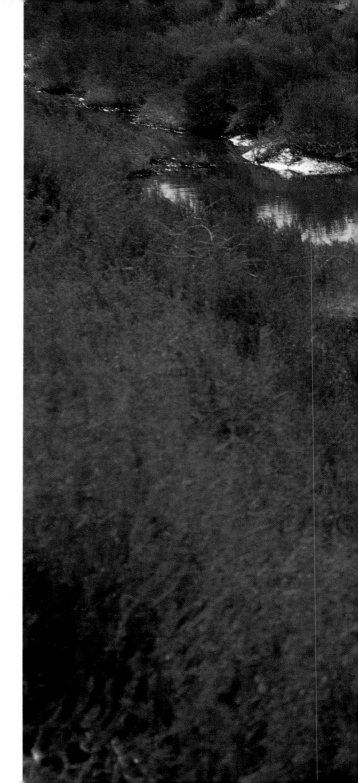

Published by Wordsong
Boyds Mills Press, Inc.
A Highlights Company
815 Church Street
Honesdale, Pennsylvania 18431
Printed in China

Publisher Cataloging-in-Publication Data
Yolen, Jane.
                    Water music : poems for children / by Jane Yolen ;
Photographs by Jason Stemple.—1st ed.
[40]p.: col. Ill.;   cm.
Summary: Original poems based on water in its various forms.
HC ISBN 1-56397-336-7
PB ISBN 1-59078-251-8
1. Water—Juvenile poetry. 2. Children's poetry. [1. Water—Poetry. 2. Poetry.]
I. Stemple, Jason, ill. II. Title.
811.54—dc20 1995 CIP
94-79163

First edition, 1995
First Boyds Mills Press paperback edition, 2004
The text of this book is set in 20-point Berkeley Book.

10 9 8 7 HC
10 9 8 7 6 5 4 3 2 1 PB

For David, picture perfect
—J.Y.

To my mom for making this possible
—J.S.

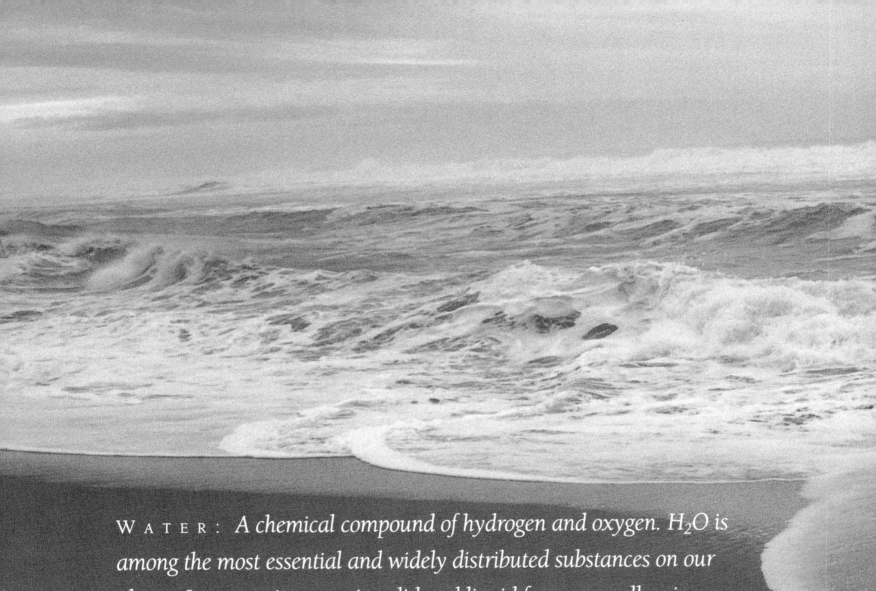

WATER: *A chemical compound of hydrogen and oxygen. H_2O is among the most essential and widely distributed substances on our planet. In nature it occurs in solid and liquid forms as well as in gaseous states. It can be snow or ice or steam, in ocean or lake or stream, in rain or sleet or tears. It is found in the cells of plants and animals, and is essential to them for nutrition.*

Contents

Reflection

Water is a magic mirror
Showing earth and sky,
Revealing the fairest
To the careful eye.

What is up is down,
What is far is near;
A truth so fragile
Only eyes can hear.

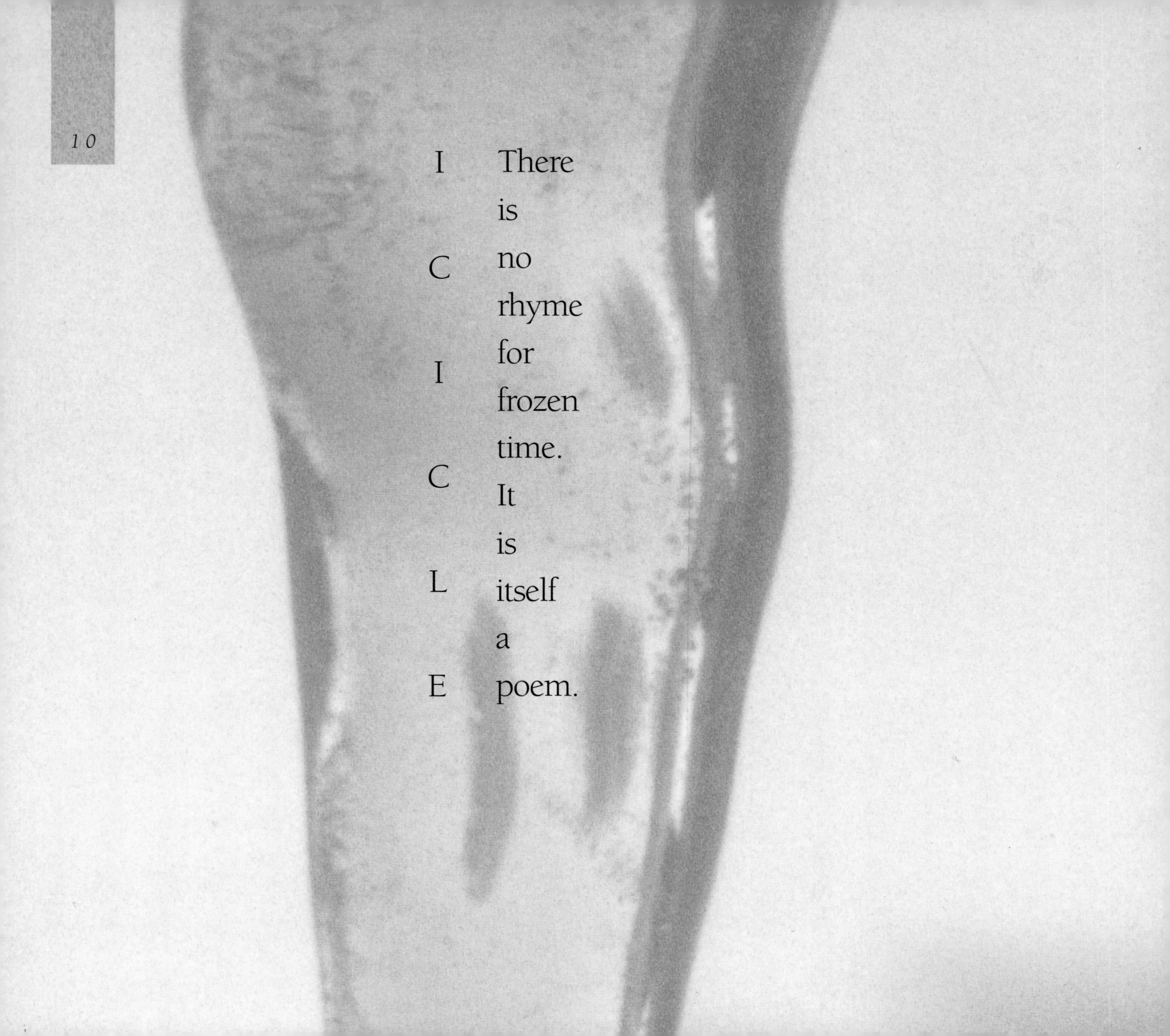

ICICICLE

There
is
no
rhyme
for
frozen
time.
It
is
itself
a
poem.

The Rock Cries Out

"And the rock cried out, 'No hiding place.'"— *Old Spiritual*

As if I were fool enough to hide
Where the casual fury of the incoming tide
Flings its angry waves upon the shore.
A dog might crouch behind that rock,
Seeing only the foam at its feet,
Too late to dodge the killing blow.
But often punished, we two know
There is no hiding place.

Take my hand. We will run along the shore
Where no water, no wave, no raised fist
Will trouble us
                anymore.

Water Jewels

How well bedecked the weeds become
When dressed in water gems.
They wear rain jewels upon their leaves
And raindrop diadems.

Waterfall

Waterfall.
Waterf a l l.

Leaves and sticks and twigs and a l l.

A rumbling, tumbling, cataracting fool
Falling over and over and over and o v e r

Into its own quiet

    Pool.

Water Lily

Pond lotus, open up your face
So sun and sky can soon erase
The pinched reserve night pressed upon it.
Dainty in your morning bonnet,
Trimly in your gown of white,
Waken from the close of night.
Tidy in your toiletry,
Water lily, welcome me.

Embroidery

On this green loom,
In this wet place,
The ocean makes
Fine water lace.

Each patterned wave
Lays down a thread
Upon the ground
Of ocean bed.

Enduring
It shall never be,
This water lace
Embroidery.

Observation

Above, blue sky
Shouts a plangent lie;
But the whisper of water
On velvet leaves
Speaks a quieter truth.
Simple, plain:
Iris after rain.

Wet Eden

What is there beyond water
To a fish?
What Heaven, what Paradise,
What one wish
Besides a bit of bread,
A passing fly,
This wet Eden
Therein to live, to die.

Washing the Dog: A Haiku

The dog was filthy.
Still she shook off our soapsuds:
Bubbles in the grass.

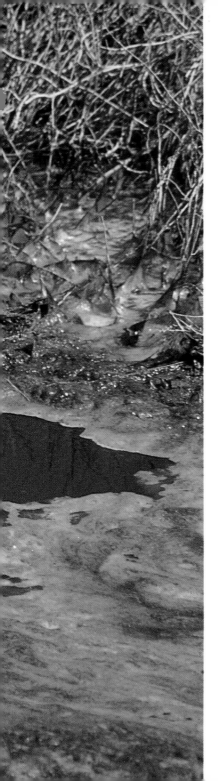

Algae

Pond scum,
Water's ghetto,
Primitive
Greengrocers.

Life.

Tangle

A muddle, a meddle
Of natural wire:
Green leaf and yellow leaf,
Stem, stalk, and briar.

Knotted and knitted
In natural angles,
A watery coverlet
Made of wet tangles.

Bath

Listen to the water
groaning through pipes
like an old woman
home with her shopping.
It complains all the way.
Filling the tub,
it settles into familiar spaces,
like that old woman sinking into her chair.
"Ah," she says, taking off her broken shoes.
"Ah," it says, the level slowly rising.
Like the woman, water has its memories
in an album of white porcelain,
where all the photos are of bubbles
and a single yellow duckie.

Washed Away: A Double Haiku

Leaf upon the land,
The wild and raging water
Washes you away.

I am such a leaf:
Too many furious words
Rip me from my shore.

Two Stones, One River

Nothing is as wise
As water passing stone,
So sure of its position
It can compromise
The path downstream,
Sometimes flooding,
Sometimes ebbing,
And sometimes running
    in between.

Water Music

"A noise of many waters"— Psalm 93

I do not hear a noise.
I hear many melodies
Where water sings across the rocks
With perfect pitch.

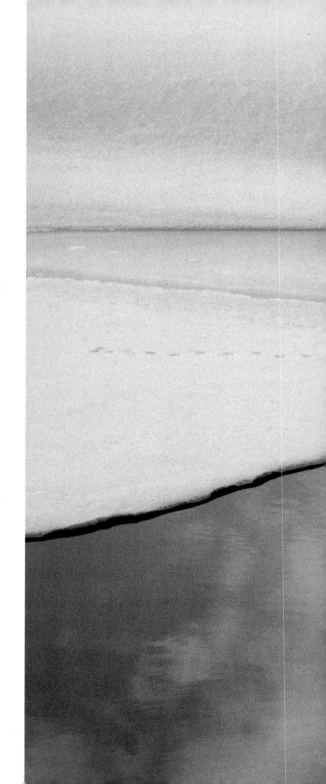

One Hundred Percent

What is *not* water
One hundred percent
Must be subtracted
From this equation.

(Cloud + ice + pond - bird = perfection)

So fly away, bird,
Become a minus
Sign.

Is it cruel to ask such accounting,
Or is it simply the mathematics
Of natural selection?

A Note from the Author

Normally a picture book grows text first and illustrations afterward. But in this instance, struck over time by the beauty of Jason's photographs, I asked him if we could do a book together. He proposed the idea of using a water theme.

So he shot many rolls of film and showed me the best of the slides. I responded poetically to the pictures he gave me. Sometimes the poems were a direct response to what was actually in the shot, but more often the photograph became a starting place for a poem that observed nature in particular and life in general.

The ice and snow photographs were taken in Colorado, in the mountains around Gunnison and Crested Butte. The ocean pictures are from the California Big Sur country. The cozy summer shots were done near my house in western Massachusetts. Water being everywhere on this planet, Jason was never without inspiration. And—after seeing his photographs—neither was I.